Emily Included

Emily Included

A True Story

Kathleen McDonnell

Second Story Press

Library and Archives Canada Cataloguing in Publication

McDonnell, Kathleen, 1947-
Emily included / by Kathleen McDonnell.

ISBN 978-1-926920-33-7

1. Eaton, Emily—Juvenile literature. 2. Children with
disabilities—Canada—Juvenile literature. 3. Children with
disabilities—Education—Canada—Juvenile literature. 4. Inclusive
education—Canada--Juvenile literature. 5. Mainstreaming in
education—Canada—Juvenile literature. I. Title.

HV890.C3M35 2011   j362.4083'0971   C2011-904504-4

Edited by Gena Gorrell
Designed by Melissa Kaita

Lyrics to "Three Rows Over"
used with the kind permission of Bobby Curtola

All photos courtesy the Eaton family
Photo on page 44 © the Toronto Star
Cover article © the Toronto Star

Printed and bound in Canada

*Second Story Press gratefully acknowledges the support of the Ontario Arts Council
and the Canada Council for the Arts for our publishing program. We acknowledge
the financial support of the Government of Canada through the Canada Book Fund.*

ONTARIO ARTS COUNCIL
CONSEIL DES ARTS DE L'ONTARIO

Canada Council   Conseil des Arts
for the Arts   du Canada

Published by
SECOND STORY PRESS
20 Maud Street, Suite 401
Toronto, ON M5V 2M5
www.secondstorypress.ca

May 1993

Emily waited by the front door in her wheelchair, while her mother called her brothers from the bottom of the stairs.

"Boys? What's going on up there?"

"Be right down," said Peter, Emily's oldest brother. "I'm just doing up Bryan's tie."

"We need to get going. We can't be late!"

The Eaton house was usually in a flurry of activity in the morning, as everyone got ready for work or school. But today was a very important day, and things were more hectic than usual. The two boys came bounding down the stairs, and Emily laughed when she saw Bryan, her youngest brother. He was ten, and she could tell by the look on his face that he wasn't one bit happy about wearing a suit and tie.

But this was not a day for jeans and sneakers. They all had to look their best. Emily was wearing her good plaid skirt and a white blouse with tiny buttons. For once, she was the first one ready. Well, almost ready – except for the cornflower blue headband her mom had bought specially for today.

Emily's father came in from outside, where he had been waiting with Mark, the middle brother. "Looks like everybody's good to go," he said. "Let's get in the car." He gestured to Mark, who sprinted into the house to push Emily's wheelchair.

Wait a minute! Emily wanted to shout, as Mark wheeled her out the front door. *I'm not good to go!*

Didn't anyone notice that she didn't have her headband on? Couldn't they see? So much fuss about the boys and their neckties, but today was all about Emily. Everybody would be looking at her – and she wanted them to see her in her new blue headband.

It was so frustrating not to be able to talk!

As her dad lifted her from the wheelchair into the back seat of the car, Emily let out a loud screech. He was so startled that he almost lost his balance, but he held on tight to Emily. She could tell he was about to launch into one of his lectures about not using her loud voice. But before he could say anything, Emily's mother spoke up.

"Hold on, Clayton. I think I know what she's upset about."

She hurried into the house and came back carrying something. At first all Emily saw was a blur, but as her mother came closer Emily recognized the curved object dotted with tiny roses of cornflower blue silk.

"Sorry, sweetie," her mom said as she stretched the headband over Emily's hair. "We almost forgot it."

Emily let out a sigh of relief. Now she felt ready to go to the hearing and meet the people who might turn her whole life upside down. They were called the Special Education Tribunal, and they were going to decide whether Emily could stay in her grade two class at Maple Avenue School, or whether she would have to leave her friends and go to some strange new school.

CHAPTER 1
A Regular School

Maple Avenue School was such a big part of Emily's life that she couldn't imagine what it would be like without it. She still remembered the very first time her parents had taken her there, to meet the principal, when she was five years old.

Back then, she wasn't even sure she wanted to go to a regular school. Ever since she was a baby, Emily had gone to the Granville Children's Centre, where all the kids had disabilities. They went to Granville for physiotherapy, speech therapy, playtime, and special celebrations like Halloween. She was used to going to Granville. But Maple Avenue was the kind of school her brothers went to. What would it be like? What did kids do there?

On that first visit, as her father pushed her wheelchair down the long hallway, they passed rooms filled with kids. Some were quietly reading or writing at desks. Others were talking and working together at tables. There were shelves of games and sports equipment, and the walls were covered with colorful artwork. In one room, Emily saw children standing around a piano, singing loudly as a teacher played for them. The sound of their voices sent ripples of excitement through her body. She wanted to be one of those kids. She wanted to stand at the piano and sing at the top of her lungs.

This place was really different from Granville!

When they arrived at the office, the principal greeted them and asked Emily's parents about her condition. They told him that Emily had cerebral palsy, because her brain had not had enough oxygen during her birth, and she had had seizures in the first few days of her life.

"Cerebral palsy isn't just one condition,"

explained Emily's mother, Carol. "It causes different problems in different people. In Emily's case, her body is 'floppy' so she doesn't have much control over her movements. And she can't see very well, because her eyes don't focus together."

Emily's father, Clayton, spoke up. "When she was a baby, her doctors said she would never be able to sit up or walk or feed herself. One doctor even tried to tell us she would be like a vegetable! But we refused to believe all that. We were determined not to limit her possibilities."

"It was difficult when Emily was born," Carol added. "Peter was only five, Mark was three, and Bryan was just nineteen months old – still a baby himself. It was a struggle to explain her condition in words they could understand. But as they got older, the boys learned to treat her like any other kid. They play with her, they read her stories, they sing to her."

Emily listened as her parents explained the progress she had made. Despite the doctors' predictions, by the time she was eighteen months old she

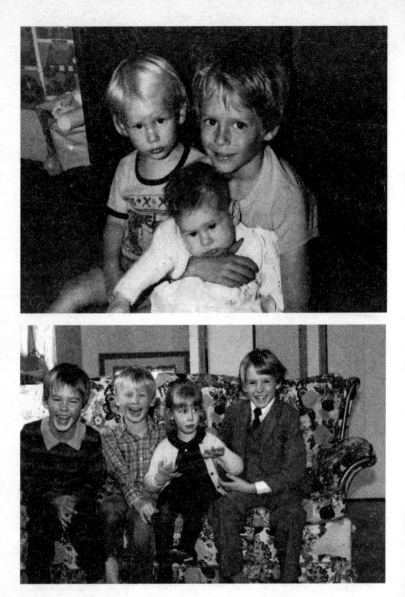

Peter was only five when Emily was born. Mark was three, and Bryan wasn't even two. It was hard for them to understand her condition at first. Before long, though, the boys treated her just like any other kid.

could sit up. By the age of three she could eat with a spoon, and hold her own drinking glass. Using a walker and special leg braces that helped her stand up, she could even walk short distances. But she still needed a lot of assistance to do things that were easy for most kids her age.

"There's a school for children with disabilities in our area," Clayton explained, "but we would rather send Emily to Maple Avenue. We think she'll learn more with classmates who are not disabled. For example, she's been trying to learn sign language. She'll be encouraged to use it more if she's surrounded by kids her own age who can speak."

"We understand that Emily faces a lot of challenges," Carol said. "But look how much progress she has already made. She deserves a chance to learn as much as she can, however much that is."

Clayton pointed out that putting Emily in a regular class would also be good for the other children, because they would learn about people with disabilities. "We want our daughter to live in our world, and be part of our community. The children she grows up with will be part of her community when she's an adult. They need to get to know her, and she needs to get to know them. The best place for that to happen is at school."

The principal nodded, but he looked a little puzzled. "Wouldn't it be simpler to send her to the school where your boys go?" he asked.

"We considered that," Clayton explained, "but it's a French immersion school, and that would be too complicated for Emily. We very much want her to come here to Maple Avenue."

The principal considered all this for a moment, and then asked, "What about Emily herself? How does she feel about it?"

"Why don't you ask her?" said Carol.

"But I thought she didn't speak…."

Clayton smiled. "Oh, she has ways of letting people know what she thinks."

The principal turned to Emily. "Would you like to come to our kindergarten, Emily?" he asked. "Do you think you'd be happy here?"

Emily remembered the kids singing around

the piano. She took a sharp breath in, then let out a sigh so loud that the principal was startled.

"That's what she does instead of nodding her head," said Clayton.

"Well, I'll take that as a yes!" the principal said, with a laugh. "Emily can come here on a trial basis. After a year, a committee for students with special needs will review the situation and decide whether she can continue here. But" – he looked at Emily – "I'm afraid you can't start right away. We will have to hire an educational assistant to help you get around the school, and we might need to make a few changes so your wheelchair can get around too. So you'll have to be patient, Emily. I'll let you know as soon as everything's ready."

While her parents thanked the principal and everyone shook hands, Emily's head was buzzing. She was coming to this school here, with all those other kids? She didn't want to be patient. She wanted to start right away!

CHAPTER 2
Way to Go, Emily!

Emily looked up, squinting in the bright sun, and tried to fix her eyes on the red object shooting across the grass. Chasing after it was a small, curly-haired animal, barking loudly. Emily had no trouble recognizing her dog Toni, but she couldn't quite make out the red thing. What was that?

It was Saturday, a perfect spring day, the first time they were able to go out without jackets. Emily and her brothers had already been outside for more than an hour. Mark pushed Emily in her blue three-wheeler while Bryan rode alongside them on his bike. The Eaton house was on a country road, with open fields around it and farmhouses and barns in the distance. Besides Toni they had another dog, two cats, and a dozen rabbits they raised in cages in the garage.

Many weeks had gone by since the visit to Maple Avenue, and Emily was eager to start school. Every time her mother had called the school, the staff had assured her that everything would be ready for Emily "soon," but no one seemed to know just when that would be. Her parents were starting to wonder if they had gotten her hopes up for nothing.

But today, as she raced headlong down the road, the wind striking her face in the brilliant sunshine, school was the furthest thing from Emily's mind. Finished with riding their bikes, the boys wheeled her across the large lawn in front of the house and hoisted her into the sandbox. Mark sat down beside her.

"Look, Emily. It's raining sand."

He held up a yellow plastic strainer he'd filled with sand. Emily grinned, watching the grains flow through the tiny holes in the strainer. It really did look like rain.

Mark noticed her grin and filled the strainer again.

"See? I can make it rain sand."

She held her hand underneath the strainer to feel the ribbons of sand cascading down. She liked the strange, almost ticklish sensation it gave her.

She looked up. There it was again, the red object. As it rolled lazily toward the sandbox, she was able to make out what it was. The new soccer ball. Of course! She heard Bryan calling behind her.

"C'mon, let's get a game going. I'll be on Emily's team."

She felt Bryan's arms wrap around her chest and lift her out of the sandbox. For a moment her legs dangled in the air, with her shoes just touching the grass. Then Bryan's grip loosened a bit, and she fell softly into a sitting position.

"Here, Bry, I'll take her."

Emily was glad to feel herself held up by another, stronger pair of arms. It was Peter, who was tall enough to carry her so that her feet didn't drag. Together, as a unit, the two of them began making their way across the lawn, toward the red soccer ball. A couple of times her legs buckled underneath her, as they sometimes did. But Peter waited patiently, holding Emily upright while she carefully uncrossed her limbs and once again took slow, deliberate steps.

"Kick the ball to me, Emily," Bryan said, standing a few feet in front of her.

She tapped the ball with her left shoe. It rolled toward him.

"Okay, I'm on your team, so I kick it back to you." He gave the ball a light kick. "Here it comes!"

She saw the red blur rolling toward her and willed her body to meet it. But her foot wouldn't respond, and the ball came to a stop in front of her.

"Whoops!" Mark called over to her. "Try again, Emily."

This time she tried to kick with her right foot, which swung right past the ball.

"Go on," said Peter. "Try again."

After three tries, she finally gave the ball a solid whack. The boys erupted in cheers. Even Toni barked excitedly.

Emily heard a voice coming from the house. Clayton was standing in the doorway.

"Hey, that's some fancy footwork! Who's the new player, boys?"

Emily threw her head back and laughed. She loved her dad's way with words, his ability to make a joke and give her praise at the same time.

He came out of the house carrying Emily's walker.

"Here, Striker. Try it on your own."

Peter guided her over to the walker. He held her up as she raised each of her hands to the bar and gripped it tightly. He and Clayton stood on either side of the walker as she began to push forward, lifting one leg, then the other. Deliberately, she made her way to the soccer ball. Moving on her own, with the help of the walker, seemed to give her more control over her legs. She gave the ball a good, hard kick, sending it shooting across the lawn.

"Way to go, Emily!"

"Atta girl!"

Just then their mom poked her head out the door. "Who's hungry?"

The three boys turned away from the rolling ball and shouted in unison, "Me!"

They went in and sat down to a lunch of grilled cheese sandwiches with ketchup. When Emily finished hers, she pointed toward the jug of apple juice in the center of the table.

"You want a drink?" Carol asked her. "Do you remember the sign?"

Emily's parents usually set aside time at meals to practice signing with her. Her brothers had to ask and say "please" too. But they could speak, while Emily had to use signs. Now she lifted one hand, as if she were holding a glass, and tipped it toward her face.

"Good, Emily."

Her mom poured some juice into a cup and helped Emily guide it to her mouth. She drained the cup and reached toward the platter, which held some extra slices of cheese. Carol held her hand back firmly.

"Ask if you want more, honey."

Emily gave her mother a quizzical look. The "drink" sign was easy, but she couldn't remember the sign for "more."

Carol held up both hands with her palms facing inward, and brought the tips of her fingers together. Then she guided Emily's hands in the same motion.

"Don't forget the other sign, Emily," said her dad from across the table. "The one that goes with it." He held one hand against his chest, moving it in a circular motion.

"The sign for 'please,'" Carol prompted her. "You put them together like this." Once more she brought her fingers together, then put one hand on her chest and made the same circular motion as Clayton.

"See? 'More, please.' Go ahead, try it."

Emily raised both hands and tried to face her palms inward, but her left wouldn't turn toward her. Then she pressed her fingertips against each other, but they didn't come together neatly, the way her mother's had.

Carol nodded approvingly. "Good try."

Emily found the sign for "please" even more difficult. She tried moving her hand in a circle, but the best she could do was brush it up and down a few times on her chest. There were so many signs to learn, and it was hard to get the hand movements just right.

"Just do your best, Emily," said Clayton.

The phone rang and Carol went to answer it. Emily tried to sign "please" a couple more times, then her father slid the plate over so she could take a slice of cheese.

"That's fine, honey. You have your own way of saying things, don't you?"

Carol hung up the phone and bounded back over to the table.

"Guess who that was?" Her voice was filled with excitement. "The principal at Maple Avenue School. Emily can start kindergarten next week!"

"That's fantastic news," said Clayton.

While Mark and Bryan cheered, Peter spoke in a newscaster's voice. "News bulletin! After months of deliberation, it's official: Emily Eaton is going to school!"

It's true, she thought. *I'm really going.*

She was excited, and more than a little bit scared.

CHAPTER 3
Hand over Hand

Maria took Emily's hands and gently bent her fingers around the handles of the rolling pin. They were in the art room at Maple Avenue School with other grade one students, all sitting at long tables, working on their projects. Maria placed her own hands over Emily's, and together they moved the rolling pin back and forth over the clump of play dough, flattening it into a smooth round.

It was over a year since Emily had started going to Maple Avenue School, and for the first few weeks she'd found it a big adjustment. Before that, the only kids she had seen on a regular basis were her brothers and cousins, and the children at the Granville Centre. Most of the people in her life had known her since she was a baby. They understood why she couldn't talk, why she sometime drooled, and why she needed to use a wheelchair. But at Maple Avenue Emily found herself surrounded by strangers for the first time in her life. She wasn't used to being treated as if she weren't there, to people talking about her as if she couldn't see or hear them. Emily often wondered if coming to Maple Avenue had really been a good idea after all. Maybe she'd be better off at a special school, where all the kids were like her.

But little by little, things got better. Emily began to feel more as if she belonged.

"Don't press too hard, Emily," Maria said. "You don't want to squish it. See, it's starting to look like a real pizza."

A couple of kids from the next table came over to see. "Hey, that looks good enough to eat, Emily," Maria smiled. She was Emily's educational assistant. There was no way Emily could manage going to school without a full-time helper like Maria to push her wheelchair, take her to the bathroom, and help her with activities like this.

As her parents had hoped, being around kids her own age encouraged Emily to do more, to try to keep up with the others. During the first month of kindergarten, she took her first steps without the walker. At first she was able to walk only a short distance on her own, but as she practiced she got better and better.

Signing was still difficult for Emily, but she found that the other kids quickly got used to her odd way of making signs. In fact, they often understood what she was trying to say better than Maria did. In the playground, the older kids figured out that Emily could go down the slide as long as there was someone sitting right in front of her. Every day at recess, kids took turns helping her up the slide and guiding her to the bottom. Emily loved the feeling in the pit of her stomach as she whooshed down the slide.

In the art room, Emily discovered quite a few

things she could do by herself. She loved finger painting, as well as using a brush, though her hand quickly grew tired from gripping the brush. One of her paintings, full of bold reds and golds, was on the "brag door" at home, the fridge door where the Eaton children put things they were proud of, like artwork and sports ribbons.

Much of the time, though, Emily wasn't able to do the same activities as her classmates, and that was where Maria came in. She and Emily did many activities "hand over hand," as they were doing now with the play-dough pizza. Doing things hand over hand with Maria meant that Emily didn't just watch what the rest of the class was doing – she did the activity right along with them, and felt really involved in what was going on. She was just as proud of the things she made with Maria as of the work she did on her own.

Because of her condition, Emily often had to take a short nap in the afternoon, and sometimes one in the morning too. She also had occasional seizures, when her heart would pound, her eyelids would flutter, and a startled look would come over her face. Although a seizure could be scary for the other children to watch, her parents reassured the school that once it was over, Emily was fine. As Carol wrote in the Communication Book:

> When Emily has a seizure, we help her relax as much as possible. We remove her to a quiet place and hold her snugly in our arms and tell her that she is okay. Usually it doesn't take more than a minute or so for her to come out of it and return to normal.

The Communication Book was something that Emily's parents had set up with Maria at the start of grade one. Unlike most kids, Emily couldn't talk about her day. The book let her family know what had happened at school, so they could talk about it at dinnertime. There was another advantage to the Communication Book. It gave Emily's parents a way to answer questions that came up in the classroom.

One day Maria wrote:

Today the students asked, "What do things look like to Emily? How far can she see?"

Carol wrote back:

We believe that Emily can see distances about the same as other children her age. What we don't know for sure is how she understands what she sees. We don't know if she sees double, or if things look bigger or smaller than they do to other people. Emily's eye problems affect her ability to communicate, too. One of the main ways we understand people is by looking at their faces, especially their eyes. But Emily can't always make eye contact when she wants to, so it's hard to "read" her. In time she might be able to use some kind of communication device. For now she really appreciates her classmates' efforts at learning to sign with her.

The grade one kids put away their art projects and went back to their classroom for music practice. They were getting ready to perform in a marching band at the school fair in a couple of weeks. Most of the class was learning to play "Oats, Peas, Beans, and Barley Grow" on the recorder, with some kids playing the snare and bass drums.

"Everybody's got something to play except Emily," Christine pointed out.

Emily and Christine were friends from kindergarten, and Emily was glad they were both in the same class this year.

"Emily doesn't mind," said Maria. "She enjoys listening too."

"I know what!" Christine suddenly burst out. "She can play the triangle."

"Hey, that's a great idea, Christine," said Maria. She turned to Emily. "What do you think about that?"

Emily took in a sharp breath and let it out with a sigh. Both Maria and Christine understood that this was her way of saying yes.

Christine ran to the closet where the instruments were kept, and came back with the silver triangle. Holding it up by a loop of rope, she stood next to Emily's wheelchair and made some rhythmic *ping!* sounds with a slender metal bar. Emily smiled, enchanted by the bell-like rings.

Christine held out the metal beater. "Here, Emily, you try."

Maria wrapped one of Emily's hands around the metal bar and brought it up to the triangle.

Ping!

With Maria guiding her hand, Emily kept tapping on the triangle. She missed it a few times, but mostly she hit it.

Ping! Ping!

Grinning with delight, Christine held up the dangling triangle for Emily. She kept on playing and, as her confidence grew, she tightened her grip on the beater. Maria loosened her own hand and, a few moments later, took it away altogether.

Emily kept beating on the triangle. *Ping! Ping! Ping!* Now she was making the sound all by herself!

Maria signaled to the rest of the class to strike up the band, and they launched into "Oats, Peas, Beans, and Barley Grow." As Emily played along on the triangle, she thought back to that first visit to Maple Avenue, when she'd watched the children singing around the piano. She had wanted so much to be one of them, and now she was.

This was why she wanted to go to a regular school.

CHAPTER 4
Everybunny Is Somebunny

Up until now, Emily's birthday parties had always been with her family – parents, brothers, grandparents, aunts, uncles, and cousins. Now she was about to turn seven, and her parents suggested a party with her school friends. Emily said yes right away, but then she began to worry. Would her school friends have a good time? Would they even want to come?

It was Bryan who came up with the idea for the bunny theme, one night at dinner. Emily responded with a loud sigh, and everyone realized it made perfect sense. So much of their family life revolved around raising rabbits. Though they were normally kept in cages out in the garage, the boys often put several bunnies in a box and brought them inside for visits. Clayton always said that he never knew when a cute furry creature was going to suddenly appear at his feet.

A few days later, Emily and Carol set to work making the invitatons, cutting them out of light blue construction paper in the shape of bunny ears. The next day, Emily took them with her to school, feeling a bit nervous and shy. She was glad to see each girl's eyes light up when she handed her an invitation.

"Thanks, Emily," said Sonia as she opened hers. "This sounds like it's going to be really fun."

The big day finally came. As the guests arrived, Carol placed a pair of furry rabbit ears on each girl's head, then attached a sheet of paper to her back with a safety pin.

"This is for the first game," said Carol. "It's called 'Everybunny Is Somebunny.' The point of the game is for each girl to guess the rabbit character pinned on her back. You each get to ask ten questions but they can only be answered 'yes' or 'no.'"

Stephanie raced over to look at what was written on Monica's back, then pulled Becky and Christine over so she could whisper in their ears. The rabbit ears on the girls' heads shook as they huddled together, laughing. The paper on Stephanie's back read "Thumper," Becky's said "March Hare," and "Peter Cottontail" was written on Christine's.

"Who am I?" Monica shouted, but she knew there was no way the others would tell her.

As the rest of the guests arrived – Sonia, Teresa, Daphne, Fatima, Emily's cousin Amanda – a babble of voices rose up as the girls tried to guess their rabbit characters.

"Come on, give me a clue!"

"No clues!"

"Only 'yes' or 'no' questions!"

Fatima managed to guess hers in only two questions.

"Am I a character in a book?"

"Yes."

"Am I in more than one book?"

"Yes."

"Am I Rabbit from *Winnie the Pooh*?"

"Yes!"

As the guessing game continued, Sonia bounded over to Emily.

"Your ears have gone crooked, Emily," she said. "I'll straighten them for you."

She gently brushed Emily's hair out of her eyes and adjusted her headband so the rabbit ears stood up straight again. Emily liked Sonia. She was one of the quiet kids at school, but she was always one of the first to help with anything the teacher asked. And she was especially good to Emily.

Soon everyone had either guessed her character or used up her ten questions. Except for Emily, whose sheet was tucked into the back of her wheelchair, where the others couldn't see it.

"Emily already knows her bunny, but the rest of you have to try to guess its name," Carol told the group. "She'll let you know when you get it right."

"We'll give you a clue," said Clayton. "It's the end of one day, and the beginning of another."

After a few moments of bewildered silence, several of the kids shouted, "Midnight!" at almost the same time. Emily grinned and let out a loud sigh, so they knew it was the right answer. But they were still puzzled.

"Who's Midnight?" asked Christine.

"It's not a rabbit you've heard of before," Clayton said.

"You'll understand later," said Emily's brother Bryan, with a mischievous grin.

Next was a singing game, one they all knew well:

Little Rabbit Foo Foo, hopping through the forest,
Scoops up the field mice, bops them on the head.

As they sang, each guest used her index and middle finger for rabbit ears and made a hopping motion with her hand.

Down came the good fairy and she said,
"Little Rabbit Foo Foo, I don't want to see you
Scooping up the field mice, bop them on the head."

The girls all pretended they were holding magic wands and waved their arms around. Emily joined in, wagging her index finger back and forth as if to say "no." In the song, the good fairy tries to persuade Little Rabbit Foo Foo to be good, but the rabbit keeps bopping field mice on the head.

"I gave you three chances," said Carol, playing the good fairy. *"Now I'm going to turn you into a goon. Zap!"* She called out to the group, "What's the moral of the story?"

"Hare today, goon tomorrow!" everyone shouted in unison, laughing.

After that they played Pin the Tail on the Bunny. When it was Emily's turn, several of the girls helped blindfold her and spin her in the wheelchair. They guided the chair toward the big rabbit poster tacked to the wall.

"Touch the rabbit and point to where you want

35

to the tail to go," said her mother. Emily brushed one hand over the poster a moment, then stopped.

"Are you sure this is where you want it, Emily?" asked Sonia. Emily replied with a loud sigh for yes and Sonia guided her other hand to pin the tail to the spot. Then Carol removed her blindfold and Emily burst out laughing. The other girls giggled, too.

She had pinned the tail smack on the end of the rabbit's nose!

After the games, Clayton helped Emily sign "Come friends, eat cake" while Carol and Bryan went into the kitchen to light the candles. Fatima followed them to see if she could help, and recognized one of the objects on the fridge door.

"Hey, that's Emily's painting."

"Yeah," said Bryan. "That's our brag door."

They all sang "Happy Birthday to You," and Emily blew out the candles on the bunny-shaped cake one by one. After that came the opening of the gifts – some finger paints from Sonia, a stamp pad set from Daphne, a bunny troll from Amanda.

The excitement of the party and opening the gifts began to wear Emily down. She started chewing on a sheet of wrapping paper, the kind of thing she sometimes did when she was exhausted or upset. Her parents had hoped she would grow out of it by now. They thought perhaps she kept doing it because it was one of the few bodily actions she could control.

"Emily, please don't chew on the paper," said her dad. Emily gave no sign that she had heard him, and kept on chewing. Clayton asked her again to stop, and this time he could tell she was ignoring him on purpose.

"It looks like Emily's getting pretty tired, and right now she's not in the mood to do what I ask her to," he told the group. "But maybe she'll listen to you girls. Could you ask her to please stop chewing on the wrapping paper?"

Clayton had expected the girls to speak to Emily. But instead they all made the sign for "stop" by holding their hands at right angles, and most of them remembered to add "please" by making circular motions around their hearts.

Emily looked at them and felt a bit sheepish. She loved the way they all launched into signing without being prompted. Until that moment, she hadn't really appreciated what an effort her school friends had been making to learn to sign.

She let the sheet of wrapping paper fall onto the coffee table.

Clayton caught Emily's eye and signed a silent "thank you" her way.

The party was drawing to a close, but there was one big surprise left. The front door opened and Peter, Mark, and Bryan marched in, carrying a cardboard box. They set it down in the middle of the guests and, with great fanfare, opened the lid. When the girls saw the cluster of baby rabbits, they shrieked with delight.

One by one the boys took the squirming bunnies out of the box: a fuzzy white named Fritz; Ginger, who was brown; silver-colored Sylvia; and Hickory, Lilac, and Dandy, who were all white with black patches on their ears, nose, paws.

"This is Emily's favorite," said Mark, lifting the

last one, a jet-black baby rabbit, out of the box. "You already know its name, don't you?"

"Midnight!" shouted several of the girls.

He put Midnight on Emily's lap, where it curled up as she stroked its soft fur.

For days afterward, Emily basked in post-party glow. Now her classmates had been to her house and met her family. Her party was still the main subject of conversation at school, and the bunny theme carried over onto the playground, with frequent rounds of "Little Rabbit Foo Foo." Something had changed. Emily could feel it. The girls weren't just her school friends anymore. They were her friends, period.

CHAPTER 5
An Honest Disagreement

Toward the end of grade one, Emily began to sense that something was going on – some kind of disagreement between her parents and the school.

One afternoon she was surprised to see her mother standing in the doorway of the classroom. Carol explained that she had just come from a meeting with the principal. Emily was usually driven home in a special van, but today her mother drove Emily home herself. On the ride home, Carol said nothing about what she and the principal had talked about. To Emily that seemed odd, because her parents made a point of including her in discussions about school. She also noticed that her mother seemed distracted and troubled. It wasn't until a few weeks later that she found out what had happened at the meeting.

When Emily first started at Maple Avenue, the principal had stressed that it would be up to the committee for students with special needs to decide whether she could stay at the school. The day that Carol had met with the principal, he had told her that the committee members had decided Emily's needs could not be met in a regular classroom. They had recommended that she go to a special school for disabled children, where she would get more individual attention.

Carol and Clayton were surprised and upset by the committee's decision. They knew that their daughter's disability made many extra demands on the staff at Maple Avenue. But they were convinced that it was good for Emily to be around children who were not disabled. She was making real progress in her signing, and in her physical abilities, too.

Just as important, Emily was happy. She'd formed a strong circle of friends. Maple Avenue had become a place where she felt she truly belonged. How would she react to switching schools?

Over the next few weeks her parents tried to persuade the members of the committee to change their minds. But after many meetings and discussions, nothing had changed. Carol and Clayton could no longer put off telling Emily what was going on. One night at dinner, they explained that the committee had decided that Emily should go to a special school for disabled children.

It was immediately clear from the look on Emily's face that this news was very distressing for her. Her brothers were upset, too.

"Why should she have to change schools?" said Peter. "She wants to stay at Maple Avenue. Don't you, Emily?"

Emily tried to make the sign for "yes" but she was too agitated.

"That's what we think, too," their father said.

"We're having an honest disagreement with the school about what's best for Emily."

"Isn't there anything we can do about it?" Mark wanted to know.

Their mother explained that they could make a formal request to something called the Special Education Tribunal to challenge and possibly reverse the committee's decision. But that would be a difficult process, she said, and they would need help. They'd learned about a place in Toronto called ARCH, the Advocacy Resource Centre for the Handicapped, that offered legal help for cases like this.

A few days later, Carol and Clayton drove into the city with Emily to meet Anne Molloy, a lawyer at ARCH. Emily liked Anne right away. Usually, when she met people for the first time, they spoke only to her parents. Sometimes they acted as though Emily weren't even there, which made her angry. But throughout the meeting, Anne spoke directly to Emily and included her in the discussion. At one point she showed Emily a photo of

Even though they knew it would be difficult, Emily and her parents decided to challenge the decision that she could not stay at her regular school.

her daughter, who was just two years old. Emily grinned and made a loud sigh of approval when Anne asked if she would like to meet her little girl someday. The Eatons spent a couple of hours in Anne's office, talking about Emily's experiences at Maple Avenue, and explaining why they wanted to challenge the school board's decision to move her to another school.

Anne told them that ARCH was interested in starting a test case based on the Canadian Charter of Rights and Freedoms. Since the Charter guaranteed equality for people with disabilities, ARCH wanted to argue that the school board was legally required to include Emily in a regular classroom just like other kids, and to provide the support she needed.

Anne warned them that although their appeal to the Special Education Tribunal could be important in advancing the rights of people with disabilities, it would be a long and difficult process. The school board's lawyers would try to show why Emily didn't belong at Maple Avenue.

Things would be written and said that Emily and her family might find hurtful.

Anne turned to Emily and asked, "Do you want your parents to go to court so that you can stay at Maple Avenue School?"

Emily thought a moment. She had no doubt about what her answer would be, but she wanted to let Anne know that she had come to the decision on her own, and how strongly she felt about it. With fierce determination, she thrust out her hand and tightened it into a fist. It was a movement that didn't come easily, but she managed to pump her fist downward, as if she were pounding on an imaginary slab of wood.

It was the sign for "yes."

"Emily, that's the fiftieth time in a row!"

Bryan was exaggerating, of course. Emily hadn't really asked him to rewind the tape fifty times – it just felt that way.

It was summer and the school year was over. Their parents had decided that the boys, who were now fourteen, twelve, and ten, were old enough to babysit, with Peter in charge. This afternoon Carol and Clayton had gone to Toronto for another meeting with Anne, and Emily was driving the boys crazy. She kept asking them to rewind the tape to the beginning of "Three Rows Over," her current favorite song, about a boy who is distracted by a pretty girl in school who sits "three rows over and two seats down."

Emily had first heard the song a week earlier, when the whole family had attended a concert at the county fair by the singer Bobby Curtola. His music, with its catchy choruses and bouncy rhythms, was just the kind she loved. After the show they had bought her a cassette tape of his greatest hits. Listening to the tape brought back memories of the fair – eating cotton candy, riding the Ferris wheel, laughing and screaming with her brothers on the bumper cars, painting a T-shirt at the Wearable Art booth.

The boys decided they had to do something to distract their sister's attention from the tape player.

Mark found a big empty box and tied a rope around it.

"Look, Emily!" he said. "We made a car for you."

They lifted her inside the box and began to tow her all around the house. Emily laughed with giddy delight, especially when the box took a sharp turn. After a while the boys found themselves back in the same fix – Emily didn't want them to stop pulling her around in the box-car.

Finally Peter had an idea. He took off for the barn and came back moments later, carrying another box lined with straw. Inside was a litter of newborn bunnies, only two days old. They were tiny and their eyes were still shut tight. Their parents were Ginger and Midnight, so one was jet black and the other two were fawn-colored. Ginger had covered the straw with some of her own hair.

The boys helped Emily out of the box-car and onto the couch. The bunnies whimpered as Peter put the box down next to her, so she could reach in and stroke their coats. They didn't have much fur of their own yet, but to Emily it felt like velvet. Peter lifted the black one out of the box and tucked it into the collar of her blouse. She giggled as it nestled next to her skin, squirming and tickling.

Summer was coming to an end. In a couple of weeks she'd be entering grade two at Maple Avenue School. The Tribunal hearing was still months away, but her parents had assured Emily that, in the meantime, everything would stay exactly the same.

But Emily was nervous and a bit scared. Hadn't the school said they didn't want her back?

CHAPTER 6
Racing Buddies

Emily held out the bag of pretzels to Freddy, who was first in line in front of her wheelchair. Meanwhile, Maria placed another bag on Emily's lap, ready for her to hand to the next person.

At the start of grade two, Emily had been given the task of handing out snack bags for the school's fundraising project, and she was proud of the job she was doing.

"Do you remember the sign for 'thank you,' Freddy?" Maria lightly touched the fingertips of her right hand to her lips, then moved her hand downward in Emily's direction. Freddy tried to imitate the movement, but the way he did it, it looked as though he were blowing Maria a kiss. The other kids in the line pointed at him and snickered. His face went red with embarrassment.

"Not to me, Freddy. You're thanking Emily, remember?" Maria prompted him. "Now Emily, you sign 'you're welcome' back to him."

Emily lifted her right hand toward Freddy and tried her best to bring it back toward herself in a sweeping motion. Maria's back was turned to Freddy, but Emily could see that he was making clumsy sweeping movements too. Stung, she realized he was making fun of her signing. One of the older girls in line glared at Freddy and motioned for him to stop, which he did. His teasing brought back the painful feelings Emily had had when she first came to Maple Avenue, when nobody knew her and she felt like an outsider. But it wasn't like that anymore, she reminded herself. Now she belonged. She had good friends, and people who stood up for her, like that girl in line – whose name she didn't even know!

Later that morning, the grade two students were divided into groups to do projects on endangered species. Each group was to choose an animal that was endangered and do a presentation about it. Emily was in a group with Tommy and Carrie, who showed her photos of different animals to help her choose. Maria reminded them to do it slowly.

"Remember that Emily can't focus on any one thing for very long, so make sure she gets a good look at each animal."

Emily's eyes opened wide when they got to the picture of a small, gray, furry creature.

"I think Emily picks that one," said Carrie. "Do you?"

Emily signed an emphatic "yes."

"I bet you chose it because it looks like a rabbit," said Tommy. "But it's really a hyrax."

No one in the class had ever heard of a hyrax. Emily, Tommy, and Carrie went to the school library to do research, and learned that, despite its small size, the hyrax was actually a close relative of the elephant. They found a map of Swaziland, a country in southern Africa, and decided to use it to show the class where the animals lived. As they worked, the three of them got excited about making their presentation, which was scheduled for the following week.

The next day Emily was sick and had to stay home. At first her parents thought it was just a cold, but then it got worse. It became clear that she was developing a severe chest infection and would have to be hospitalized. Emily was deeply disappointed at having to miss doing the hyrax presentation with Carrie and Tommy. She had to stay in the hospital for more than two weeks, and ended up being absent for a whole month of school.

By the end of November Emily felt well enough to return to class. On her first day back, she discovered that Maria was working in another classroom, and a new person, Cheryl, had been assigned to be her educational assistant. Emily was surprised and unhappy about the change. She and Maria had been together since grade one, and they knew one another so well. Emily felt that Cheryl was much less patient with her than Maria had been, and she didn't try to help her do things hand over hand. To make matters worse, Emily was still recovering from her illness, and grew tired more quickly than before she got sick.

Once again, Emily began chewing on things, and making noises. She didn't mean to disturb the rest of the class, but when she got too loud Cheryl would take her out of the room. This happened more and more frequently, often several times a day, as Emily's parents saw from Cheryl's notes in the Communication Book. Clayton wrote back to her:

> Emily's noises are sometimes a problem for us too. We think it happens when she is upset about something, and that she is trying to express herself in the only way she can. At home, we try to deal with it by asking her to use her "soft voice." We explain that there are times when it's okay for her to use a loud voice, but that this isn't one of them.

To add even more to Emily's problems, the school board officials, who were preparing their case for the Tribunal hearing, had told Cheryl to try to measure how much Emily was learning. At times, it seemed to Emily that giving tests was the most important part of Cheryl's job. Day after day Emily was asked to identify different colors, parts of the body, and other things. After a while she got bored with the endless round of tests. It was frustrating having to answer the same simple questions over and over. Sometimes she got so fed up that she deliberately gave a wrong answer.

At times like this, Bobby Curtola's song would often pop into her head. The bouncy melody always cheered her up, but there was something in the lyrics that drew her too. Everybody thought she identified with the cute little girl in the song. But sometimes Emily felt like the singer, as if his words were expressing her own feelings and frustrations.

I just can't seem to concentrate
I can't buckle down

I never get my school work done
My head's always turning around.
I catch the teacher's angry looks
When my head's not buried in my books.
She knows my thoughts are all around
That girl three rows over and two seats down.

Through the winter, Emily grew healthier and stronger. She had always loved going outside on cold, sunny days. After a big storm, with snowdrifts piled high around their house, her dad would set out on his cross-country skis, pulling Emily behind him on a toboggan. And there were school outings to the municipal rink, where her friends took turns pushing her wheelchair around the ice.

As winter turned to spring, Emily and Clayton began training for the annual Spring into Action race. They had participated in many running events, including the Terry Fox run to raise money for cancer research. But this was a competitive race with a special section for runners pushing wheelchairs. Now that Emily had a new racing chair, Clayton figured that this year he and his "racing buddy" had a good chance of winning a trophy.

On weekends Emily looked forward to their practice runs. They would get up early, just the two of them. Clayton would make them a light breakfast and they would set out along the country roads just as the sun was peeking over the horizon. Toni usually sat on the chair's footrest, yapping loudly at Emily's feet. After a few minutes, they would break into a sprint and Emily would scream with delight, exhilarated by the sensation of the world whizzing by. The whole run took an hour – sometimes more if they stopped to chat with neighbors. Each time they took a different route, but as Emily began to notice familiar landmarks along the road, she felt a bit downcast, knowing that the run was almost over and they would soon arrive back home.

Whenever they passed a herd of cows, Clayton would slow down so Emily could watch them. She loved the sound of their mooing, and the way their tails brushed back and forth as they grazed. One time, as they were jogging beside a field of corn

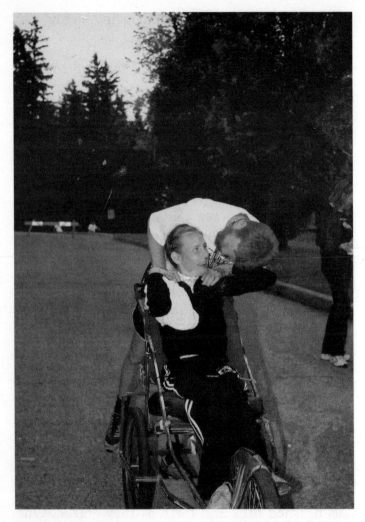

Emily and her dad practiced every weekend for the Spring into Action race in her new racing wheelchair.

seedlings, Emily heard some screeching noises. She looked over to see a huge flock of birds roosting in the field. The noise grew to a loud roar as the birds took flight all at once.

"See the long necks on those birds, Emily?" said Clayton. "Those are sandhill cranes. There must be more than a thousand of them! They're on their way north to their breeding grounds."

Emily watched them as they soared higher and higher. For a few moments she felt a restlessness, a powerful longing to burst out of her wheelchair and fly alongside them.

On the day of the race, the air was cool and crisp. Right from the crack of the starter's gun, Emily and Clayton pulled into the lead, and Emily realized that all their training had paid off. As they ripped around the course, at times she felt as though her wheelchair was about to lift right off the ground and vault into the air. She remembered the sandhill cranes.

This is what it must be like to fly!

They approached the finish line, and Emily saw

crowds of people on either side, clapping and cheering. She was the first racer to cross the finish line. The next day, she and her dad had their picture in the local paper. It showed a grinning Emily holding the trophy, engraved with the words "Wheelchair Racer Section: First Place."

CHAPTER 7
The Tribunal

Emily looked out the window and saw a flash of red zoom past their car. She let out a groan to get her brothers' attention.

"Hey, there's one we almost missed," Mark said. "That's number sixteen. Good thing you caught it, Emily."

They were counting the red cars on the road, and Emily had become so absorbed in the game she'd completely forgotten how upset she'd been over her cornflower blue headband. When they pulled into the parking lot next to the long gray building, though, the thought suddenly came to her: This was the day they'd been building up to for so long. They were finally here, at the Special Education Tribunal hearing.

Once inside, they met Anne, the ARCH lawyer, and followed the signs to the meeting room. Anne had said that the Tribunal hearing would be much like a trial, but this plain room didn't look anything like a courtroom. There were several rows of folding chairs on either side, with two tables in front of them. Anne and Janet Budgell, another ARCH lawyer, sat at one table, while the lawyers for the school board sat at the other. At the very front of the room was an even longer table, where two men and a woman sat. They must be the members of the Tribunal, Emily realized – the people who would decide her future at Maple Avenue. She wondered what was going through their minds as they watched her family file into the front row of chairs. Couldn't they understand that she just wanted to go to school like any other girl her age? She knew it wasn't that simple, but she still wondered why there had to be all this fuss about it.

First there was some talking back and forth between the lawyers and the Tribunal members, which Emily found boring. But soon Carol was called to take a seat up front, next to the long table.

"Wish me luck," she whispered to Emily.

The man sitting in the middle chair at the long table, who seemed to be in charge, asked Carol to raise her right hand. "Do you swear to tell the truth in the testimony you are about to give?" Emily's mother nodded solemnly and said, "I do." Emily realized then that the hearing was quite a bit like a trial, after all.

Carol had prepared an opening statement to give the Tribunal members a glimpse of Emily's life and who she was as a person. She spoke at length about Emily's birth, her difficulties as an infant, and her eventual diagnosis of cerebral palsy. Emily was proud of her mother, of how well she spoke and how poised she was during the long series of questions from the lawyers.

"Emily has very strong likes and dislikes. She loves music, and books about animals. She can be a bit of a fussy eater – she's not crazy about pizza, and with hot dogs she's only interested in the bun. The one thing she'll always eat is a grilled cheese sandwich with ketchup," said Carol. "Which makes her pretty much like any other eight-year-old."

A ripple of laughter went through the room. Even the Tribunal members, who until now had maintained blank expressions, broke into smiles.

After Carol's testimony, each of Emily's brothers was called up to make a short statement. All three of them were a bit nervous about speaking in front of so many grown-ups. But it was their chance to show the Tribunal that, to them, Emily was a normal kid who belonged in a regular classroom with other kids her age.

"When Emily comes home from school, she's always happy and eager to tell us about what she's done that day," Peter told the Tribunal.

"I can be in a regular class," Bryan said. "So why can't Emily?"

Next to give statements were the parents of three of her schoolmates. Emily was surprised at how strongly they felt about their daughters' friendship with her. "Before knowing Emily, I was afraid of handicapped people," Christine's mother told the Tribunal. "I didn't know how to act around them."

Sonia's mom wiped a tear away as she spoke. "I want my daughter to be in the same class as Emily – not just for Emily's sake but for Sonia's, too."

As the morning wore on, Emily felt a combination of pride and embarrassment at listening to so many people talk about her. It was a bit strange, hearing her own name over and over.

After a break for lunch, it was her father's turn to speak. Like Carol, he made an opening statement, then answered questions from Anne and the lawyers for the school board.

Anne asked him to explain why he and Carol felt so strongly about keeping Emily in a regular classroom.

"Our community includes Emily's neighborhood school," Clayton said. "And the people who live in our community, the children that she will grow up with and who will be part of her community when she's an adult, go to that school. They need to get to know Emily now. We can't bring her back at the end of her school career and plug her into that community. She has to be there now, so she can grow up with those children and those children can grow up with her."

Everyone was silent. His words seemed to have struck a chord.

In the late afternoon, the hearing was adjourned until the next day. Emily couldn't imagine what more there was to say. As far as she was concerned, everything the Tribunal had heard so far should make their decision a simple one.

But there was much more to come, Anne said – at least two more weeks of testimony. There were many other witnesses for both sides, and each side would present evidence to support its case. Emily knew that the witnesses for the school board would argue that, since she couldn't be tested on what she was learning, Emily didn't belong at Maple Avenue. She was glad she wouldn't be there to hear any of that. It would just make her feel like an outsider all over again.

Since Emily and her brothers were at school during the day, they weren't able to attend any more of the sessions. But either Carol or Clayton went every day. They were encouraged by Anne's skill in challenging the school board's case. The board's lawyers stressed the difficulties of having a disabled student like Emily in a regular classroom. But in her questions, Anne reminded them of the benefits of having Emily in the class – for her and for the other students.

Most evenings, Anne came to the house to talk over the day's events with Emily and her parents. Since she had to be at the courthouse first thing every morning, Anne stayed at a nearby hotel. But she usually phoned home while she was still at the Eatons' so she could say good night to her daughter. One night, after Anne got off the phone, it looked to Emily as though she was crying. Emily could see how much Anne missed her little girl, and she wished she could comfort her. As Anne passed her wheelchair, Emily held out her hand. Anne took it and squeezed it while she wiped her eyes with her other hand.

"Thanks, Emily," she said. It was the kind of moment that meant so much to Emily, when she was able to make herself understood without words.

During the Tribunal hearing, Anne arranged for a great deal of testimony from expert witnesses – professors, doctors, and researchers who had special knowledge of disability and education. Often in the evenings, Anne brought the expert witnesses over to the house to meet Emily and the rest of the family. There was one witness who made a deep impression on Emily. His name was Bob Williams. He was the director of a disability agency with the United States government, and he flew in from Washington, D.C., especially for the hearings.

Anne wanted Emily and her parents to meet Bob before he appeared at the hearing. It was a lovely day, so they all gathered on the lawn outside his hotel. When Emily was introduced to Bob, she was astounded to see how much he was like her. Of course, she knew many people who used wheelchairs, and several who had cerebral palsy. But she'd never met anyone quite like Bob Williams. He too had cerebral palsy, and his symptoms were very similar to hers. He couldn't speak, and he had poor control of his muscles. He even drooled the way she did!

Yet Bob did have a way of talking. Attached to one arm of his wheelchair was a computer-like screen with a keyboard, where he typed words that were translated into sounds. Emily was fascinated by the way this communication board gave him a voice. She listened intently to his every word.

Bob planned to tell the Tribunal about his own childhood, how being in a segregated class had damaged his self-esteem. "As a child in the special class, I knew that my teachers and others had few expectations that I would do anything in life."

He had also suffered bullying and discrimination. "Because they never had the opportunity to get to know me as a person, some kids used to call me a 'retard' and pelt me with stones."

Bob's words hit Emily like a shocking blow. At times she'd felt ignored or excluded by her classmates, and she'd been the subject of hurtful teasing like Freddy's. But she'd never experienced the kind of outright cruelty that Bob was describing. As he spoke, it became clear that he had endured this kind of treatment many times when he was growing up. Once he learned to use the communication board, and was able to put his thoughts into words, he noticed that people treated him differently, and took him more seriously. But with or without the communication board, he knew that, inside, he was still the same person.

"People think that because a person can't speak, they don't have anything to say," Bob said. "But you and I know that's not true, don't we?" He fixed his gaze on Emily as he said this.

"You understand so much more than you can say, Emily. You need the people around you to realize that, don't you?"

For a moment Emily felt as though he could see right into her soul, that he understood her in a way no one else could. Her parents and brothers tried their best to read her thoughts and feelings, but even they got it wrong much of the time. Bob knew what it was like. He'd felt that intense longing to communicate – to express his feelings, to speak his thoughts, to be heard – and the deep frustration of not being able to.

He reached out and took Emily's hand.

"It's like you want to tell the world, 'I'm here. Don't give up on me!'"

Suddenly overcome with emotion, Emily burst into tears. But she kept a tight grasp on Bob's hand. He'd spoken the words she could not speak for herself. It was a moment that, without realizing it, she had been waiting for all her life.

After a few weeks, the Tribunal hearing ended. The Eatons were confident that Anne had argued their case as forcefully as possible. Now all they could do was wait for the decision.

One evening the phone rang. Emily heard her mother pick up the phone and say, "Oh hello, Anne." Emily was excited. Maybe it was the news they were waiting to hear!

Then she heard Carol's voice drop very low, and she realized the news must not be good.

"We lost," Anne told Carol. "The Tribunal agreed with the school board. They said that Emily should be moved to a special class for disabled students."

They had even said that Emily's parents were not doing what was best for her, Anne went on. By fighting to keep their daughter at Maple Avenue, Carol and Clayton were treating Emily as a symbol rather than a person, according to the Tribunal.

It was crushing news. Now they faced some difficult decisions. Anne said that if they challenged the Tribunal's ruling at the next level up – the Divisional Court of Ontario – it would take months for the case to come to court. In the meantime, Emily might have to change schools. How were they going to break the news to her? How would she react?

Carol and Clayton now had to deal with new doubts and questions. Was it worth it to go on fighting? Was it true, as the Tribunal had said, that they were doing the wrong thing for their daughter?

What really was best for Emily?

CHAPTER 8
An Amazing Day

At the end of grade two at Maple Avenue, Emily faced an uncertain future. The Eatons had decided to continue the case, so Anne had filed an appeal of the Tribunal's ruling. But the Divisional Court hearing was several months away. What would happen at the end of summer break, when it was time to go back to school? Emily did all she could to put these worries out of her mind.

It turned out to be a wonderful summer. She learned to swim with water wings at the local pool, and discovered the delicious freedom of being completely on her own in the water. Her signing kept getting better and better – she could now sign more than a dozen words without any hand-over-hand help. As they usually did in August, the whole family made the trip to the county fair, where Emily got to watch people shearing sheep and milking goats. On a platform near the animal pens, there was a woman spinning yarn from raw sheep's wool. Emily was transfixed by the whirring of the spinning wheel, by the way it turned so fast it seemed to disappear.

They left the animal pens, and Emily noticed that they were heading toward the big open-air stage. As Carol pushed Emily's wheelchair, Mark and Bryan kept looking back at them and whispering. When Emily saw Clayton put his finger to his lips, urging them to be quiet, she wondered what was up.

They found several empty seats on the center aisle, and removed one to make room for the wheelchair.

"I was hoping we'd get seats closer to the stage," said Carol. "I had no idea there would be such a crowd."

"Must be some pretty big name who's perform-ing next," said Clayton, winking at the boys.

A voice came over the loudspeaker: "Ladies and gentlemen, please put your hands together for Bobby Curtola!"

As the singer bounded onto the stage, Emily's parents and brothers watched to see how she would react to the news that her favorite singer was about to perform.

Bobby made his way to a microphone stand near the edge of the stage, while an electric guitarist and a drummer took their places behind him. But instead of launching into his first number, Bobby hopped off the platform and headed down the cen-ter aisle, followed by a technician unwinding an extra-long cord. He stopped just in front of Emily's wheelchair, lifted the microphone to his lips, and turned toward the audience.

"Folks, I'd like to introduce you to a remarkable young person. Her name is Emily Eaton, and she has to deal with some tough challenges in her life. But with the help of her family and friends, Emily does a lot of the same things you and I do. She plays soccer, she goes to school every day, she even competes with her dad in wheelchair races. A little bird told me that this is one of her favorite songs, and I'd like to sing it for her right now."

Bobby signaled toward the stage. The drummer struck up a rhythm, and a familiar run of chords sounded from the guitar.

There's a girl in school that I adore.
She's a cute little girl five feet four.
She's got a personality the talk of the town.
She sits three rows over, and two seats down.

The song ended, and the audience exploded in applause. Bobby kneeled down next to Emily's wheelchair so the two of them could pose for a photo.

"As soon as we get a print, I'll autograph it and send it to you. How's that, Emily?"

She beamed as Bobby gave her a kiss on the cheek. He returned to the stage and launched into

Kathleen McDonnell

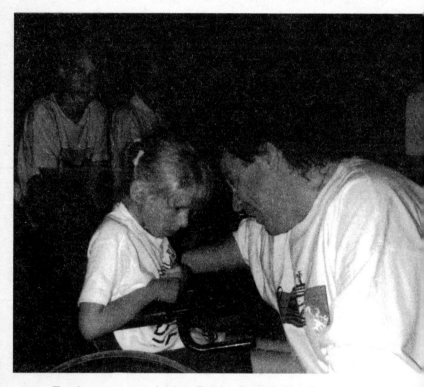

Emily was stunned when Bobby Curtola, her favorite singer, left the stage to sing to her.

78

his next number, but Emily was buzzing with so much excitement that she barely heard the rest of the show.

As they all headed out afterwards, Clayton said, "That was amazing. I had no idea he was going to come down and introduce Emily."

"Yeah," said Peter. "How'd he know about you racing with Emily and all that stuff?"

"I can't imagine," said Carol.

They all turned to look at her. The three boys shouted at once.

"It was you!"

"You knew all about this, didn't you!"

"Why didn't you tell us?"

Carol only grinned.

"See, Emily?" said Clayton. "You weren't the only one who was surprised!"

CHAPTER 9
A Matter of Principle

"Bingo!"

Carrie raised her hand and waved it around enthusiastically. The grade three class at Maple Avenue School was playing Vowel Bingo, and Carrie's card won the first round. Laurel, Emily's new educational assistant, was helping her play her card hand over hand.

Emily thrust her hand out and tried to imitate Carrie's triumphant shout. Laurel shook her head, making her long silver earrings sway back and forth.

"No bingo yet, Emily," said Laurel. "You still don't have anything under 'U.'"

"U-sixty-five," called Tommy, starting the next round.

Emily put her hand up and again tried to call out, which made Laurel laugh.

"Emily, you little monkey!" she cried. "I know you're just trying to trick us into thinking you have bingo."

To everyone's relief, Emily had been allowed to return to Maple Avenue that fall. The school board had agreed that, until the Divisional Court made its ruling, she could continue in grade three with a full-time educational assistant. Emily was relieved that she could stay at Maple Avenue with her friends. But there was still the constant worry in the back of her mind: what would happen when the Divisional Court made its ruling?

Getting used to working with Laurel was also hard for Emily. There was so much more to the assistant's job than just physical tasks, like putting on Emily's leg braces and helping her go to the bathroom. Emily needed someone who would get to know her as a person, and help her learn as much as she could.

Fortunately, Laurel was young and very open to ideas. In the Communication Book, Carol mentioned that Emily liked to have a special "name sign" for the important people in her life. Laurel came up with the idea of the letter "L" signed at ear level, because Emily was so fascinated by her earrings. Before long, Emily started to feel as comfortable with Laurel as she had with Maria.

As the school year progressed, Laurel looked for more ways to include Emily in classroom activities. Every day during silent reading time, she asked one student to read quietly to Emily on the carpet, while the rest of the children read at their desks. The kids were eager to volunteer for the job, and it was a good way for them to get practice reading aloud. Emily especially enjoyed it when they read funny books like *Mortimer* and *The Paper Bag Princess*, and she loved hearing original stories that they'd written themselves.

Laurel found other ways to involve Emily in

what was going on. When students needed extra help with math or spelling, Laurel worked with them one-on-one at Emily's desk. After a while the gatherings around her desk became part of the day's routine, and pushing her wheelchair became the most sought-after job in the classroom.

Emily loved all the activity and attention, but at times it became too much for her. When she was tired or frazzled, she made loud outbursts, and from time to time she grabbed and scratched the people around her. The other kids found this very confusing.

"What's wrong with Emily?" they asked Laurel. "Why is she mad at us?"

"I don't think Emily really means to hurt anyone," Laurel explained. "But sometimes she gets upset when there's too much going on around her."

"Then we should figure out some ways to include her that don't stress her out," one of the boys spoke up. "Right, Emily?"

Relieved that her classmates were beginning to understand, Emily let out a loud sigh to show that

she liked his suggestion. Once they got to thinking about it, the kids started to come up with all
kinds of ideas. During drama exercises, one group
decided to act out a "city life" scene in which Emily
played a character who tripped and fell on the side-
walk, while the others played characters who had
different reactions to her predicament. Another
time, during gym class, the kids took turns pretend-
ing they were bulls while Emily acted as matador,
waving a dark red towel. At first Laurel was wor-
ried that Emily would get upset with all the noise
and activity. But she had a wonderful time, giggling
as each bull charged her wheelchair. Bit by bit, the
class was figuring out how to involve her without
wearing her out.

Laurel wrote all this in the Communication
Book, as well as other activities she knew Emily's
family would enjoy hearing about.

Today we played soccer, using Emily's
walker on the grass. She kicked the ball
and laughed when I told her she was

playing like her brother Peter. After practicing kicking skills, she got back in the wheelchair and I pushed it to the closest goal post. Emily and I buddied up and played goalie. We made three saves!

Carol wrote back:

Wow! You always give us so much to work with — thanks!! It is so helpful to know what Emily is anxious to share with us when she gets home from school.

In February the Eatons learned that the Divisional Court of Ontario had ruled against them and upheld the Tribunal's decision. This time the family felt much better prepared for the news. Anne had told them that no matter what the Divisional Court decided, it wouldn't be the end of the struggle. Emily's case would almost certainly go on to the next level, the Ontario Court of Appeal.

In the years since they had first decided to challenge the school board, Emily's case had received far more attention than they had ever imagined. It was no longer just about whether Emily would be allowed to stay at Maple Avenue School. Most people who worked on disability issues believed that denying Emily the right to be in a regular classroom was a form of discrimination, and a violation of her rights. The Canadian Charter of Rights and Freedoms states that "Every individual is equal before and under the law and has the right to the equal protection and equal benefit of the law without discrimination and, in particular, without discrimination based on race, national or ethnic origin, colour, religion, sex, age or mental or physical disability."

Disability rights groups all over the country were watching Emily's case closely. Several organizations had applied to the court to be "interveners" in the case, which meant that their lawyers could present arguments that might influence the final decision.

Although the school board was allowing Emily to finish grade three at Maple Avenue, grade four would be another matter. The school would no longer provide a full-time assistant for Emily, and her parents would have no choice but to look for another school for her.

One way or the other, Emily would be leaving Maple Avenue at the end of the school year.

CHAPTER 10
A Loud, Clear Voice

Emily woke up. She was lying on something soft and comfy. But she wasn't at home in her bed. Then she remembered: she was at school, on the reading couch.

That was what the kids called the couch in her classroom at Blessed Sacrament School. When Emily had started at Blessed Sacrament, Bill, the grade four teacher, had borrowed a couch from the vice-principal's office for her to nap on during the day. But it also became the spot where other students read books aloud to Emily, so they started calling it the reading couch. It was supposed to be only for Emily and whoever was reading to her, but sometimes one or two other kids snuggled up beside Emily to listen too. Bill decided this was okay, on two conditions.

"As long as the couch doesn't get too crowded," he told the class. "And you only get to listen to Emily's book *after* you've done your own silent reading."

At first, Emily had been so upset about having to switch schools that she had refused to listen when her parents tried to talk to her about it. Carol and Clayton had heard that Blessed Sacrament, which was a twenty-minute drive from their home, had a policy of including students with disabilities in regular classrooms. They had set up an interview with the principal and Bill, who would be Emily's teacher, to discuss the challenges Emily faced and the problems they had encountered at Maple Avenue. When Clayton mentioned that Emily had often been removed from the classroom when she made loud outbursts, Bill spoke up right away.

"When Emily makes noises," he said, "I'll bet

she's trying to communicate something. If she's taken out of the room whenever she tries to use her voice, what kind of message does that send – to her and to the rest of the class – about her worth as a person? It's up to us, the adults, to set a good example. There's got to be a better way to deal with this problem."

Clayton and Carol looked at one another with relief. That was just the kind of response they had hoped for. They went home and told Emily all about Blessed Sacrament. They were so excited about her new school, and especially about Bill being her teacher, that this time Emily couldn't help but listen.

A new situation was always a huge adjustment for Emily. But Bill made her feel welcome, and his attitude encouraged the other students to get to know her. There was something about the reading couch, especially, that made the change much easier than she had expected. By the end of the first week, Emily was already feeling at home at Blessed Sacrament.

From her spot on the reading couch, Emily could see several students closing their books. Silent reading was over for today, and the next period was social studies. But first, Bill said, he wanted to announce the major assignment for the next few weeks: each student would prepare a speech and deliver it to the rest of the class.

Evveryone groaned in unison.

"A speech?"

"In front of the whole class?"

"A good speech should inform and persuade," the teacher went on. "The audience should learn or discover something they didn't know before. Your speech can be on any topic you choose, as long as it expresses your own original thoughts." Instead of the usual grading by the teacher, the other students would rate the speeches on a scale of one to ten.

As Bill finished explaining the assignment, an excited buzz spread through the room as they began to brainstorm ideas. Then one girl, Tiffany, raised her hand.

"Emily won't have to give a speech, will she?"

"I mean everyone in the class," the teacher replied. "Emily included." But in fact he was caught off guard. He hadn't given any thought to how she might take part in the assignment. At the end of the day, he wrote a note about it in the Communication Book:

Of course Emily should have a chance to present a speech, too. Perhaps one of you could work on it with her, and I or one of the other students can read it aloud to the class.

In Emily's speech therapy class, she had been learning to operate a special kind of tape player. Her parents were always on the lookout for things that would give her more independence, and they were delighted to hear about a machine that might let her choose her own tapes and play them without help. When they found out that the device would only play as long as the switch was pressed down, they realized that it wouldn't be much use for playing music tapes. But when he read Bill's note, a thought occurred to Clayton: this might be just what Emily needed to carry out the assignment.

He spoke to the speech therapist about it, and she agreed to send the tape player home so they could try it. When he told Emily about his idea, she got very excited. They both wanted her speech to come as a surprise to Bill and the rest of the class.

Emily decided the subject of her speech would be "How I do things differently from most people." Clayton made suggestions and Emily accepted or rejected them. It took quite a while to work out the speech, because Emily was very particular about what she wanted to say, and turned down a number of Clayton's ideas. He wrote it out sentence by sentence, with every word subject to her approval.

Once Emily was satisfied, Clayton recorded the speech into the tape machine so that Emily could hear the whole thing. The next day he sent a note to Bill:

Emily's speech is ready and we are sending it with her today. But it's not on paper, so don't worry about finding someone to read it for her. Just take the thing with the red button out of her bag and put it on her desk. She'll do the rest.

The teacher was intrigued. At the start of each school day he wrote the name of that day's speaker on the blackboard. This morning it was Emily's name he wrote. A wave of curious comments rippled through the room.

"How is Emily going to give a speech?"

"Won't somebody else have to give it for her?"

Just before morning recess, Bill wheeled Emily to the front of the room and placed the device on the desk in front of her, as Clayton had directed. Emily reached toward the tape player and pressed down hard on the red button. There was a click as the tape began to roll. As a voice emerged from the tape, the attention of the whole class was riveted on the machine.

"I would like to speak to you today about how I

do things differently than most of you. I have cerebral palsy, which is an injury to my brain that makes it difficult for me to use my muscles. This means I need to find different ways to do many of the things we do together each day. We all like to talk to our friends. Most of us use our voices to talk with our friends, but I use my face and eyes to let my friends know what I am feeling."

There was complete silence from the students as the voice on the tape continued.

"When we go for walks on the playground, you use your legs and I use my wheelchair, but we all enjoy the sunshine. When we go to the gym, you run and jump and kick the soccer ball. I use my walker to run and jump and kick the soccer ball. But we all get lots of exercise. Most of you read books by yourself. I need to have someone read to me, but we all enjoy reading."

It took tremendous effort for Emily to hold the switch down, and several times she felt the muscles in her hand start to weaken. But she was determined to make it to the end of the tape. She thought of Bob Williams, and how his communication board had given him a voice. This was her father speaking on the tape, but the words and the ideas – those were all hers.

"In school we all must make a speech to the class. You stand at the front of the class and speak with a loud, clear voice. I sit in my wheelchair and press a switch to play the tape recorder to present my speech in a loud, clear voice."

The speech ended and Emily finally let go of the switch. The classroom exploded in applause. Everyone, including Bill, was clapping and cheering. Emily was exhausted but she felt a deep sense of joy and pride. She'd given her own speech. She'd found her own voice.

That night at dinner, Emily showed her family a sheet with the rating the class had given her speech. It was unanimous: ten out of ten.

The sheet went right up on the brag door.

CHAPTER 11
The Court of Appeal Rules

While Emily settled into life at Blessed Sacrament School, Anne was preparing the case for the Court of Appeal. The Court of Appeal is the highest law court in Ontario, and it deals only with legal issues, so no one in the Eaton family attended the hearing. Anne kept them informed about how it was going, saying that the three Court of Appeal judges seemed quite receptive to her arguments, and that she was optimistic about their decision.

Of course, since Emily had already switched to another school, the Court of Appeal's ruling wouldn't make much difference to her personally.

But the case had gone far beyond the right of Emily or any other disabled student to go to regular school. It was about the principles of equality and justice for all people with disabilities, and the Eatons were determined to see it through to the end. But they had been disappointed before, so they didn't get their hopes up too much this time.

Anne's call finally came.

"I have news," said the lawyer when Carol answered the phone. She was usually calm and collected, but now there was tension in her voice. "You better get Clayton on the line, too."

As soon as Clayton picked up the extension, Anne let out a jubilant shout: *"We won!"*

"What?"

"We won! The Court of Appeal overturned the Tribunal's decision!"

Carol and Clayton could hardly believe what Anne was telling them. The Court of Appeal had ruled that denying Emily the opportunity to be educated in a regular class did indeed violate her equality rights under the Canadian Charter of Rights and Freedoms.

She read from the decision, written by Madame Justice Louise Arbour:

"From the earliest age, disabled children should see themselves as part of the mainstream of society, and children who are not disabled should see them the same way. Inclusion into the main school population is a benefit to Emily because without it, she would have few opportunities to learn how other children work and how they live. And they will not learn that she can live with them, and they with her.

"And there's something else I want you to hear. Remember how the Tribunal criticized you for taking Emily's case to court? Listen to what Justice Arbour says about that:

I do not agree with the Tribunal's suggestion that the pursuit of Emily's legal rights to equality, by her parents who are her legal representatives, was ill-conceived and detrimental to the child...The parents availed themselves of the only procedures made available to them by the legislation."

As Anne read from the decision, Carol and Clayton found themselves overcome by emotion. They were barely listening when Anne said they should come to the ARCH office for the official announcement the next day. She had to remind them about it twice.

Emily and her parents were lucky to make it into Toronto just before a huge snowstorm closed all the major highways into the city. As they entered the building where ARCH had its offices, they were swamped by the crowd of reporters that greeted them. Several photographers swooped in to get a shot of Emily in her wheelchair, and the glare of all the flashing lights made her shut her eyes.

Anne and Janet, the two lawyers who had done so much work on the case, were waiting for them at the door of the ARCH office.

"Well, Emily," said Anne. "It looks like you're a celebrity now."

Anne waited for the reporters to assemble inside the office, then made the announcement of the decision. It was clear that most of the reporters knew the basic facts already, but Anne wanted to make sure they understood what it really meant. "This decision," she told them, "will have a strong influence throughout Canada, because it deals with the Charter of Rights, which applies to every provincial Education Act in the country."

When Anne finished speaking, the reporters turned to the Eatons to get their reaction. Suddenly Clayton found himself surrounded by a cluster of microphones.

"We're overwhelmed," he said. "It's so much more than we could have hoped for, it's almost beyond belief."

In the midst of all the excitement, the Eatons

knew that their struggle wasn't over. Anne had told them that even if they won here, the decision would almost certainly be appealed to the Supreme Court of Canada, the highest court in the country.

But there would be plenty of time to think about that later. Right now, Emily and her family wanted to enjoy their moment of victory.

CHAPTER 12
The Highest Court in the Land

As her wheelchair rolled over the shiny marble floor of the great entrance hall, Emily looked down, mesmerized by the dancing patterns of light. Sunshine was streaming through the tall windows that reached all the way to the ceiling. Before her loomed two long, curved staircases, flanked on each side by enormous stone pillars. In the center of the floor were the letters "SC" in dark blue tiles, surrounded by garlands of leaves.

Emily was now twelve years old, and it was hard to believe it had been more than four years since her family had first embarked on the case.

But they were finally here, in the nation's capital, and the case was about to be heard by the Supreme Court of Canada.

The grand entrance hall to the Supreme Court was certainly magnificent. But at the moment the Eatons were preoccupied with something else: just how were they going to get Emily and her wheelchair up into the main courtroom?

Carol stopped an official-looking man and asked if there was an elevator they could use. He thought about it a moment, then led them down a long corridor to a service elevator. They rode up one floor and wheeled Emily down a hallway, only to encounter another set of stairs between them and the main courtroom. Clearly, the Supreme Court was not the most welcoming place for visitors in wheelchairs.

Fortunately there were only a few stairs, and Clayton was able to lift the wheelchair over them. They made their way to the entrance of the courtroom. Over the doorway was a large image in stained glass of what looked like two mythical horselike creatures facing one another. But Emily only got a brief look, because as soon as they crossed the threshold, they were greeted by a flood of flashing camera lights.

Emily was the person everyone was waiting to see.

At the front of the courtroom were nine desks of dark polished wood, all connected to one another and arranged in a curved line. Behind each desk was a high-backed chair with red upholstery, and along the walls and ceiling there was dark wood paneling. Facing the nine desks were row upon row of long tables, where dozens of lawyers in black robes were milling around, talking. They were representing the governments of three provinces – Ontario, Quebec, and British Columbia – and most of the major disability organizations in the country. Among them was a new lawyer named Stephen Goudge, who was taking over Emily's case from Anne Molloy. Anne herself had recently been made a judge.

Nearest the door was the public gallery, which consisted of several rows of wooden benches.

Everyone in the courtroom turned to watch as Emily and her family made their way to the front bench, where there were seats reserved for them. The public gallery was filled with people with disabilities – many in wheelchairs, some who had the distinctive features of Down syndrome, others with guide dogs in harnesses. Emily's case was the most important disability rights case ever to reach the Supreme Court of Canada, and all these people wanted to be there to witness it. The Eatons found out later that so many people had come to the hearing that they couldn't all fit into the courtroom. Court officials had opened up a separate room where the rest of them could watch the proceedings on a large video screen.

Suddenly a voice called out, "All rise!" and the nine judges, dressed in their ceremonial red-and-white robes, marched in and took their places at their desks.

One by one, the lawyers walked up to the front and made a brief presentation. Occasionally one of the justices asked a question, or one of the lawyers approached the justices' desks. But they spoke in low murmurs and the spectators in the public gallery could hear only snatches of what they were saying.

Emily's interest faded as the voices droned on and on. She drifted off to sleep on Clayton's shoulder but soon woke, squirming with discomfort. She'd had surgery for a curvature of the spine only a few weeks before, and it was very uncomfortable for her to sit upright for long. Clayton wheeled her out of the courtroom, followed by several reporters. In the hallway, one of them asked what Emily thought about what was going on.

"She understands that it's about whether she can go to her neighborhood school or not, right, Emily?" Clayton replied. Now that Emily was in a different school, he told the reporters, the outcome of the case wouldn't affect her personally, but they were pursuing it because of the principle involved. "Emily knows that this is an important decision," he said. "Not just for her, but for all children with disabilities."

The reporters could see for themselves that this was true. They only had to look at all the people and groups who had come to the hearing. No matter what happened in Emily's case, society's view of people with disabilities was undergoing a huge change.

A few hours later, the hearing ended. The justices said they would not make a decision right away. That was disappointing after all the excitement. Even the lawyers weren't sure when the Supreme Court's ruling might be announced – it could be days, weeks, even months.

The Eatons had planned to stay in Ottawa overnight so that they could attend a session of Parliament. The next morning, as they approached the parliamentary chamber, they saw dozens of reporters clustered around the prime minister, peppering him with questions about the issues of the day. After watching the session of Parliament, the family left Ottawa to drive home. It was well into the evening before they learned, to their surprise, that the Supreme Court had released its ruling earlier that day.

While the Court felt that being in a special class for disabled children didn't violate Emily's rights, Justice John Sopinka, who wrote the decision, said that schools and other institutions should do everything possible to include disabled people. Segregating children like Emily should be a last resort.

Once again, Emily Eaton was the big news story of the day.

The family found out that at the very same time they were visiting parliament, reporters had been searching for them all over Ottawa, to get their reaction to the Supreme Court's decision.

"Just think," said Carol. "We were standing right there, so close to the prime minister, and all those reporters. And none of them had any idea who we were."

"They sure missed out on a big scoop," Clayton added, to the laughter of Emily and the boys.

The Eatons went to Ottawa to hear Emily's case at the Supreme Court. They also visited the Parliament Buildings (top).

EPILOGUE
July 2010

"It would be impossible."

Dao Ming shook her head. The petite, articulate young woman had served as the Eatons' tour guide and interpreter since they had arrived in Beijing. They had been to many parts of the city, and Dao Ming was impressed by their determination to include Emily in everything they did. But a visit to the Forbidden City? That was another matter entirely. With all those stairs, Dao Ming didn't see how they could possibly take Emily along.

The Eatons were thrilled that they'd actually

managed to make this trip to China. Emily and the boys were grown up now, and they were all busy with their own lives. So it was difficult for them to get together for one day, much less a month-long trip halfway around the world.

Emily had finished high school and lived at home with her parents. With the help of a personal support worker paid for by the government, she led an active life, going to fitness classes, yoga, art galleries, and the local library. Peter and Bryan both lived in Toronto and had jobs in the theater world, while Mark was working as a teacher in China. He was getting married to Ling, a young woman he'd met there, and the rest of the family had flown over from Canada for the wedding.

More than ten years had gone by since the Supreme Court's ruling on Emily's case. Despite the fact that it overturned the Ontario Court of Appeal's ruling, the Supreme Court decision had been a huge step forward for the rights of disabled people, and the effects were still being felt a decade later. Emily's case had helped launch a pioneering effort to include people with disabilities in all aspects of daily life.

In 2006, the United Nations had adopted the Convention on the Rights of Persons with Disabilities. It called on society to view them not as objects of pity, but as active members of society who are entitled to the same rights and opportunities as everyone else. In particular, the UN Convention strongly supported including children with disabilities in regular classrooms. A few months before the Eatons' trip to China, Canada had officially adopted the UN Convention, adding its signature to that of more than 140 other countries. The struggle for equality and dignity for people with disabilities was far from over, but Emily's case had made an enormous difference.

Since their arrival in China, the Eatons had seen very few people in wheelchairs or with any kind of disability. They had learned that most people like Emily were still living in institutions. Though the situation in China was beginning to change, people with disabilities were usually kept separate from the mainstream of society, much as they had been decades earlier in North America.

Once again, Emily became an ambassador for disability. She and her wheelchair were a subject of great interest wherever they went. People stared, more out of curiosity than rudeness, because many had never seen anyone in a wheelchair before. But they were extremely friendly and eager to help, which was good, because few buildings in Beijing were wheelchair-accessible, and the Eatons found obstacles wherever they went. The apartment they were renting, for instance, was on the fifth floor, but the building had no elevator!

So they weren't surprised that Dao Ming thought a visit to the Forbidden City would be impossible for Emily, but they assured her that everything would be fine. Somewhat reluctantly, she agreed to take them, convinced that these crazy North Americans had no idea what they were in for.

On the way there, Dao Ming prepared them for what they were going to see.

"The Forbidden City is an enormous complex built in the fifteenth century that housed the Imperial Palace of the emperors. It came to be known as the Forbidden City because only members of the royal family were allowed there. The common people were forbidden to enter."

At the imposing entrance, the Imperial Way, they came to the Dragon Pavement, a stone ramp carved with clouds and dragons, with a long staircase on either side. The members of the royal family had to walk up the steps to the palace, Dao Ming told them. "They are called the Cloud Steps," she said. "The only one who didn't have to walk up them was the emperor, who was carried up the ramp on a throne by his servants."

They started up the Cloud Steps. Clayton pulled Emily's wheelchair, tilting it backwards and bumping it up each step. They were used to dealing with stairways, but these were the deepest, widest stairs they'd ever encountered, and there were dozens of them. A hot, blistering sun beat down on their heads as they trudged up.

"Hey, Emily," said Peter. "You're getting carried up just like the emperor."

"We're going to start calling you the empress," said Clayton.

Emily burst out laughing.

When they finally they arrived at the top of the stairway, Dao Ming started to tell them more about the Forbidden City. Suddenly she fell silent. When she tried to speak, it sounded as if she had a catch in her throat.

"Is something wrong?" Carol asked her.

Dao Ming slowly regained her composure.

"No. Yes. I mean – I was wrong. I was so sure it would not be possible for all of you to come into the Forbidden City. But I see now that you refuse to accept limits, for yourselves or for Emily. She has gone everywhere with you, because you believe that she should be able to go where anyone else can go. You are a wonderful family. I am honored to be your guide to Beijing."

They were moved by Dao Ming's words – all it seemed, except Emily, who had a broad, goofy grin on her face. It was one of those times when they could tell she was enjoying something, even though they didn't know what it was.

It was her dad's joke. She just couldn't stop smiling about it.

No place in this world is forbidden to me, she was thinking. *For I am Empress Emily.*

A Message from Emily

Today I am happy to be included in my community. I enjoy shopping for new clothes, seeing a movie, spending the day at the beach, or going to a baseball game with friends. I enjoy going to see plays at the theater where my brothers work. I like to go for a run in my special running wheelchair on Sunday afternoon with my dad. I like to read books or just watch TV with my mom. I was honored to be a bridesmaid in my friend's wedding and enjoyed dancing late into the night with everyone.

I was excited to visit China and meet my new sister-in-law and her family. I enjoyed seeing all the sights in China with my family. I was very happy when people in China helped carry me to the top of all the many stairs, to make sure I could see everything. I need help from my family and friends to be included in all of these things. I am glad that the Supreme Court said that I have a right to have the help I need to be included in these activities.

I am happy that children will read my story. I am very proud that going to the Supreme Court has helped other kids with disabilities to be included in their classrooms.

Emily Eaton

Author's Note

How does Emily communicate?

All human beings have a fundamental need to share our thoughts and feelings. We tend to think of "communication" as something that is done through words, either spoken or written. But we also communicate in many other ways – through our eyes, our facial expressions, the movement of our bodies. Often these are spontaneous, natural gestures – nodding the head for "yes," shaking it to indicate "no," rolling our eyes to show we're bored by someone or something. Signing, used by the deaf and hearing-impaired, is a form of language that substitutes actions, particularly hand signals, for spoken words.

Emily participates in conversations, but because of her disability, some methods of communication are not available to her. She can make vocal sounds, but is not able to form words, and her impaired vision makes reading difficult. Emily learned some American Sign Language (ASL) when she was young but, as the story shows, it was frustrating for her, since signing requires a great deal of muscle control and precise movement.

A number of technologies have been developed to assist people who have difficulty communicating, such as the device Bob Williams uses in the story, which translates his typed words into a computerized "voice." These devices help people with disablities to adjust to our "normal" way of communicating, rather than the other way around. But not all people with communication difficulties are able to use these devices, and there are drawbacks and limitations for those who can use them. Devices cannot reproduce the natural flow of what we think of as "conversation." Many people with cerebral palsy, who speak with an "accent" that is extremely difficult for the average person to understand, still prefer using their own voices to using a communication device.

The people in Emily's life tune into her by learning to "read" her "body language" – her eyes, her sounds, her movements and facial expressions. In other words, they adapt to her way of communicating as much as possible. Of course, this has many challenges. Conversation is a two-way street. Emily wants to be understood, but, like anyone else, she also wants to strike up a conversation, express an opinion, and change the subject when she feels like it. Sometimes, according to her father Clayton, finding out what's going on Emily's mind can be a bit like a game of Twenty Questions. But when the people around her make the effort and pay attention to her particular way of communicating, Emily is able to express herself and fully participate in her world.

ACKNOWLEDGMENTS

I am grateful to Tyler Hnatuk, who originally told me about Emily's story. Our conversations about disability have helped shape this book and have broadened my thinking enormously. Thanks also to the unfailingly helpful Robert Lattanzio, for responding patiently to my many requests for research material; to Anne Molloy, for sharing her memories and offering helpful suggestions; and to Angela Valeo, for her insights.

I want to thank the young people who read the manuscript and gave me valuable feedback – Lee Rosensweet, Myfanwy Cappel, Willa Milchem

Bourne – and the somewhat older people who worked with me to make the story stronger and tighter – Gena Gorrell, Carolyn Jackson, and Margie Wolfe.

Alec, Martha, and Ivy were founts of encouragement and fun, as always.

The Ontario Arts Council provided support during the research and writing of this book, for which I am thankful.

Though some names and details have been fictionalized, *Emily, Included* is a true story. I am deeply indebted to the members of the Eaton family – Carol, Clayton, Peter, Mark, Bryan, and Emily – for welcoming me into their lives and encouraging this re-telling of their remarkable story.

ABOUT THE AUTHOR

KATHLEEN MCDONNELL is an award-winning author and playwright of adult and children's literature, including The Notherland Journeys series – *The Nordlings*, *The Shining World*, and *The Songweavers* – and *Honey, We Lost the Kids*. Born in Chicago, Kathleen lives in Toronto with her family.

Visit her website at www.kathleenmcdonnell.com

And follow her author page on Facebook